Practical Law of Attraction

How to Align Yourself with the Manifesting Conditions and Successfully Attract Wealth, Health, and Happiness

© **Copyright 2019 - All rights reserved.**

The content contained within this book may not be reproduced, duplicated or transmitted without direct written permission from the author or the publisher.

Under no circumstances will any blame or legal responsibility be held against the publisher, or author, for any damages, reparation, or monetary loss due to the information contained within this book, either directly or indirectly.

Legal Notice:

This book is copyright protected. It is only for personal use. You cannot amend, distribute, sell, use, quote or paraphrase any part, or the content within this book, without the consent of the author or publisher.

Disclaimer Notice:

Please note the information contained within this document is for educational and entertainment purposes only. All effort has been executed to present accurate, up to date, reliable, complete information. No warranties of any kind are declared or implied. Readers acknowledge that the author is not engaging in the rendering of legal, financial, medical or professional advice. The content within this book has been derived from various sources. Please consult a licensed professional before attempting any techniques outlined in this book.

By reading this document, the reader agrees that under no circumstances is the author responsible for any losses, direct or indirect, that are incurred as a result of the use of information contained within this document, including, but not limited to, errors, omissions, or inaccuracies.

Table of Contents

Introduction	1
Chapter 1: Beginner's Guide to the Law of Attraction	6
Chapter 2: Visualize, Act, and Be Grateful	24
Chapter 3: Wealth Mindset	31
Chapter 4: Health Mindset	43
Chapter 5: Success, Happiness, and Love	56
Chapter 6: Romantic Love	74
Chapter 7: How to Check If It Is Working	85
Conclusion	92
References	95

Introduction

In 1987, a struggling actor wrote himself a check. He had just moved to Los Angeles from Toronto, a world away at that time. Far from his home and family, he was poor and struggling to find his big break. After long nights of auditions, he would drive up to Mulholland Drive, park his car, and stare out at the scintillating lights of the city glimmering back at him. He would look at this city that represented all he wanted: fame, beauty, and wealth. He would turn his car off and visualize. He would envision directors recognizing his talent, his name in lights, and his face on the cover of magazines.

That dream seemed so far from that peak in Southern California. But he visualized every day, maybe as a coping mechanism or some deep delusion, but he promised himself he would make it. Somehow. One day he decided he needed an extra push. He put his money where his mouth was, or hypothetical money at least. At the peak of his poverty, he wrote himself a check for 10 million dollars. Many would call him crazy. He gave himself three years to make it happen. Due date: Thanksgiving 1995.

The years passed, and he never forgot that dream. He worked hard, twice as hard as he had before. Two days before his deadline, on November 23, 1995, he got signed to a movie contract for, you guessed it, 10 million dollars.

Today, directors write roles for him; his name is in lights, and he has been on the cover of uncountable magazines. His net worth is now more than the lofty 10 million he dreamed for himself while at the bottom. He saw it. He worked for it. He manifested it. That is how Jim Carrey claimed his success.

Do You Believe?

Jim Carrey has been practicing the law of attraction since the 80s, but this is a technique that goes back to the beginning of conscious thought. Buddha, Edison, and even Oprah have all believed in the law of attraction. But what is it exactly? You are sure to have heard, it given the success of The Secret and numerous celebrities backing the law. Its methods are simple: the law of attraction is about clearing negative thoughts and replacing them with positive ones. Through positive thoughts and the right action, you can achieve a more prosperous life. Done. You can put this book down now. But if it were that easy, then the rest of this book would only be a waste of space on your hard drive, next to photos of your friend's baby you never visit and productivity PDFs. Let's make sure this isn't a waste of space. The law of attraction is more than your thoughts, but your thoughts are transformative.

Jim Carrey's story is one of numerous examples of the law of attraction. It is the practice that states we can attract whatever we want into our lives. Newest car model? Dream it. Want a raise? Believe it. Need millions of followers? Visualize it. Whenever your mind thinks with positive intention, visualization, and consistency, you will begin to flourish.

Our thoughts, negative or positive, come into being. Be careful what you think. The law of attraction is universal energy; it flows through every creature, swims in every cell, reaches the bottom of the ocean, and beyond the sun. It is as ubiquitous and invisible as air until you notice the wind. The law of attraction is like a newborn pup: it has limitless potential and the ability to be trained. But is it that easy? Just a thought? Sometimes it feels like we have a million thoughts a second. We are constantly thinking, from the moment we wake up to when we fall asleep. How is thinking, a sometimes passive activity, supposed to bring me the life I want?

The life you want is inside of you. It isn't in the newest diet, the hottest new outfits, or the fanciest cars. Your happiness and fullest life come from within. You have had it inside of you the whole time. Like an untapped well, through this book, you will learn how to make it overflow. The law of attraction does not happen overnight or after just one mindfulness meditation session. If it did, we would all be driving a Mercedes-Benz and have the bodies of our dreams. We live in a material world, and we need to still operate in it. But all that we want is made of the same energy that we are. The following chapters will teach you how to clear the way and become in alignment with that energy. There is no telling how long your manifestations will take. What is known is that patience, faith, and consistency will become your new best friends. Ground yourself in these following words, and you will have your manifestations sooner than you could have imagined. Be patient. Stay focused. Be grateful.

What You Will Learn

In this book, we will see how the Law of Attraction has influenced numerous lives and household names. You'll learn how ordinary people on the edge of bankruptcy, suffering after airplane crashes, and wearing potato sacks to school, have managed to become some of the most influential people of our time.

Here is another story. A person has been living in a city for the last few years. They are stagnant. They have been in the same small apartment since college. The groove in the couch keeps getting bigger, as does their belly. The most impressive accomplishment they have had all year is watching *Game of Thrones* from start to finish in a single weekend. Their dating life is as dead as flowers after the first frost. Their friends and family seldom call. They wake up, go to work, get take out, come home. They live the same day on repeat like the saddest version of *Groundhogs Day*.

This person believes that the world is against them. They blame the world for where they are in their life and play the victim card at every turn. Their parents didn't love them enough. They never dared talk to their high school crush. They were too dumb to get into the college they wanted. They could never ask for a raise. They know they have a book in them but know it won't be any good. They hate running and aren't meant to be fit. The narrative this individual believes has dictated possibly years of their life. Since they never got up off the couch and believed they could make a change, they never did.

Does this sound like you? Do you feel like you have plateaued in one or several of these areas? Do you want to take control of your life and make it a more positive, loving, and successful one? Do you want to have the energy to hike mountains and find true love? Do you want to land your dream job and have an overflowing bank account? Well, you are reading the right book. In this book, you will learn about the tenets of the law of attraction. The Law is a coveted secret that has transformed the lives of those who practice it religiously. You will read how to have consistent cash flow, youthful energy regardless of your age, live a life of abundance, and find true love. Are you ready to manifest the life you have always wanted?

Chapter 1:
Beginner's Guide to the Law of Attraction

The law of attraction has been in our minds since the earliest believers in a greater universe. It is mentioned in nearly every religion and has been practiced throughout the centuries. One of the most common areas where people have already bumped into law of attraction teachings is the Bible ("How the Teachings of the Bible are Related to the Law of Attraction," 2018). *"And all things, whatsoever ye shall ask in prayer, believe, you shall receive it"* (Matthew 21:22).

Through this book, you will notice that many religious philosophies are in alignment with the law of attraction, and its origins are even older than the Bible. Its first mention was from Buddhist texts and teachings, one of the oldest and most prevalent religions. Buddhism still influences the minds and hearts of modern people. The exact origin date of Buddhism is unknown, but texts show that the development of Buddhism was somewhere between the sixth and fourth centuries BCE in India. It is the offspring of Hinduism, but with no gods and more minimalistic attire. The belief system traveled east and made a home in every Asian country. Its following has had peaks and plateaus through history like the perfectly raked ridges in a zen garden. Today, Buddhism is making a comeback. There are now large followings in Europe, Brazil, and the United States. It is possibly the oldest source that advocates for the law of attraction.

Here is one of the most famous and essential quotes in Buddhism: *Your mind is everything. You are what you think.* It is evident that the law of attraction has been in the collective consciousness since we started developing it. Many are attracted to the philosophies of Buddhism because of its focus on mindfulness. Mindfulness is the ability to be focused entirely on the present moment. Mindfulness is the practice of seeing a moment without judgment. Humans naturally judge moments and experiences. Those who practice mindfulness learn to not color in experiences with good or bad crayons; they are just moments that have passed ("History of the Law of Attraction." n.d.). The practice helps us domesticate our often wild thoughts on an expectation or reaction and has us look at the moment from an objective perspective.

This is Your Brain

Our brain is a funny place. You would think that it would want us to be happy and present all the time, right? It feels nice when anxieties or regrets are not blasting through our brains at the volume of 10 subwoofers.

However, our minds are tethered between the past and the present. The brain's main objective is to keep you safe. On our most primal level, survival is more important than growth. Our cognitive, emotional, and survival mechanisms have been around a lot longer than our conscious minds. That means that they are going to have a more significant hold on you, even though we are the only animals that can rationally think through any issues.

Although we are logical creatures, many people use their brain power to focus on what they can't control. Their minds bounce between pains of the past or fears of the future. They find it all too difficult to be here, now.

This issue makes sense from an evolutionary psychology level. Evolutionary psychologists believe that we have survived because of our ability to learn and plan. We learn from past actions, which helps us make sense of the past. We then decipher what worked and didn't work and plan the future around our lessons. This back and forth keeps people stuck between the past and the future, which makes it easy to disregard the present. Our own awareness ironically holds us back.

Today, we still need learned experience to have a smooth future, but mental monsters like anxiety, doubt, and depression lurk through our brains and prevent us from being happy now. Our brains are low-key working against us. Our base survival instincts don't want us to thrive; they want us to survive ("Why Is It Hard to Live for the Moment," n.d.).

Additionally, mindfulness allows us to control all of our thoughts. When we think something nasty, deprecating, or hurtful, we have the power to adjust our thoughts. We are not a reflection of the impulsive thoughts that bop around our brains. We are a reflection of the reactionary thought. Controlling your thoughts will be essential to mastering the law of attraction.

Scientists who study mindfulness have suggested that practicing mindfulness meditation can cage our fears around the past and future. Numerous studies show that those who can be mentally present are happier people.

Mindfulness will be a crucial component for mastering the law of attraction.

Your mind is a powerful tool. Everything that you have ever wanted is inside of you. You just had to remove your own blocks. To become more mindful, we must start meditating. Get your sitting pillows ready, because meditation will be mentioned frequently throughout this book.

Although meditation today is used for several reasons such as stress reduction, focused attention, and breathwork, its roots are in controlling your inner world. Buddhist texts understand that we are not in control of many parts of our lives, down to not having control over when we are born. The only aspect of our lives we can control is our inner world. Our thoughts, dreams, desires, biases, and judgments are all within our control. No one tells us what to think other than ourselves. Once you have a handle on your thoughts, you will have an upgraded consciousness. From there, you can start influencing your reality.

Cultivating that higher mentality takes dedication and time. But once you reshift your mindset and get on a higher frequency, you will be able to attract everything you have wanted.

The law of attraction is grounded in mindfulness. Mindfulness is going to help you shift and rewrite the impulsive thoughts. Our thoughts often leap around us as if frogs are breaking loose from a science experiment. Mindfulness allows us to keep our frogs, for the sake of the metaphor, organized, and will enable us to calmly select one at a time.

Mindfulness doesn't allow our knee-jerk ideas, thoughts, emotions, judgments, bodily sensations, current surroundings, or biases to dictate the moment. We learn to take a step back and look at the moment objectively.

Let's say you are living in a small apartment and have a roommate. You wake up, work out, and now you want to make breakfast. Your roommate is peacefully in the kitchen, chopping vegetables, and in the way of the stove. You are getting increasingly hangry and don't want to move around your roommate. You start to mentally resent them, thinking "Ugh, why are they here NOW. Don't they know that I need the kitchen too?! No please TAKE YOUR SWEET TIME." These thoughts are fueled by your need to eat, the frustration of not getting your way, and not having an ideal environment. But these are just your thoughts. When we flip the script, we can see the objective moment for what it is. What is actually happening? Your roommate is chopping vegetables. That's it.

The other component of mindfulness is being gentle with yourself. These thoughts are inevitable. We are not trained to control them and have to put in work to do so. Catch yourself when you start to mentally scream at your roommate. As long as you don't act on your thoughts, you aren't a bad person for having them. Don't beat yourself up over it. It isn't the first thought we have that counts, it's the one that responds to it. You want to be non-judgemental in the moment and of your own thoughts.

We have an estimated 60,000 thoughts a day, and it would be physically exhausting to monitor all of them at once. The ones that we catch and rephrase give us back our power. We don't want to let our thoughts run away from us.

The Power of Negative Thoughts

When you allow the negative thoughts to dictate your perception of the world, that is when we want to intervene. Negative thoughts are incredibly potent because they also attract more negative events to happen to you. Bad thoughts are bad juju.

Your thoughts are energy, and they create a lightning storm over your head. If you are stressed and focused on getting to work on time but are nervous about being late, lateness happens. You bump into traffic, get held up with construction, or find a parking ticket on your windshield. You will focus your attention on the negative parts of your ride, which might end up making you late. Negative thoughts attract negative outcomes.

Another form of negative thoughts are limiting beliefs. As we go through life, we are told narratives about what we can and cannot do. If we are poor, we will stay poor. If we are overweight, we will stay overweight. These stories that we tell ourselves limit our ability to make a change. They block our potential, like when the moon eclipses the sun—it can darken our view and true potential.

When we focus and reinforce these limiting beliefs, we stay that way. Our actions will go with the script that we have written for us because we are the stories we tell ourselves.

The first step towards the law of attraction is uprooting limiting beliefs. They block your energy path and prevent all of the positive things you want in your life from reaching you (Sicinski, 2018).

Here are some practical ways to begin shifting your negative thoughts and limiting beliefs.

STOP

When you start to hear the creeping voice saying, *Ugh, I hate it when* (insert minor frustration), think STOP. Slap it like a mosquito. Try to stop the thought before letting it finish. Some people wear a rubber band around their wrist and snap it when they have a terrible thought. They then begin to associate pain with whatever thoughts they are trying to reframe.

You can also keep a tally for a day and mark down how many negative thoughts pop up. It might make you more conscious of how frequently you think negative things when you see an army of lines on your page.

If you want to dig even deeper into your bad thoughts, write them down and see if you notice the theme. Are they about your body? How much your mom annoys you? Do you wish you could quit your job? Being aware of which thoughts come up more frequently will help you become more aware of them and can illuminate which areas of your life you feel least satisfied. Once you have them identified, you can begin to wonder where they originated.

Our limiting beliefs are often planted within us before we are conscious of them. Maybe your limiting beliefs with money are because your mom had a lot of financial worries that you overheard as a kid. Or your fear of losing your relationship is because you had a traumatizing breakup. Once you start getting to the root of the problem, you can begin weeding them out of your brain and planting positive ideas.

Positive Affirmations

If you have been practicing "thought stop," then you know which thoughts are coming up the most frequently. From there, you want to begin to reframe them or buffer them with positive thoughts. Instead of thinking, " Ugh I will never be able to get that job," STOP yourself and rewrite your story. Pause the idea from even finishing and then think of a positive reframing. "If I am qualified, I am just as good as any other candidate. I have a good chance of getting this job!"

Buffering your negative thoughts with a positive affirmation will give you confidence and will begin to remold your attitude. Just like eating vegetables every day, saying positive affirmations will make your brain healthier and stronger. It will start to see the positive parts of your life and abundance around you. The more you do it, the easier it will become. Our brains are often our biggest barriers!

Be Gentle

Telling your thoughts to stop and reinforcing them with positive affirmations, unfortunately, does not come naturally to us. If it did, there would be no point in books like this one existing. It needs to be emphasized that this is a practice. Once you become more mindful of your negative thoughts, you could end up getting more frustrated at yourself for having them! You want to be done with them already!

A way to work through these frustrations is to talk to yourself as if you were a friend. When we have a friend come to us with a problem, we seldom say, "Well, you brought it upon yourself. Also, you look terrible in that outfit. And who cut your hair? Oh, I almost forgot, you'll die alone." Friends don't talk to each other like that. If they did, the friendship would dissolve faster than Airborne in a cup of water.

You need to be gentle with yourself during this process. Talk to yourself like a friend. Be your own cheerleader!

It may feel like a lot of pressure all of a sudden to be SMILING AND POSITIVE ALL THE TIME. That isn't helpful either. You don't want to sweep your negative thoughts under the rug. You need to give them their space because they do exist or might be valid. You are allowed to feel frustrated at times. Then once you have felt your feelings, take a step back and be reflective about them. You can give them space without letting them dictate you.

If you are finding that you are just suppressing your emotions, you might need a more tangible way of letting them go.

It might mean carving out time to let it all out. Go into a field, drive in your car, or take a bike ride and shout it out. A therapy session sounds nice as well. Alternatively, you can take a piece of paper and journal out all of your negative thoughts and frustrations. Let a free-flowing stream of consciousness come out of you. Don't hold back. Whatever room you have left on your paper, scribble at the bottom furiously.

Then you can take a step back and see these thoughts, beliefs, and frustrations lie harmlessly on a piece of paper. They are no longer rattling around inside of you and are released and acknowledged.

Then destroy it. Rip the angry paper to pieces. Don't allow these thoughts to continue to exist. By getting rid of it, it begins the process of letting go. It acknowledges their existence and puts you in the right step to move forward.

When we get these mental roadblocks out of the way, our path becomes a lot smoother. Yes, there will always be roadblocks, but you will begin to know when to swerve around them or avoid them altogether.

Once you begin recognizing and defusing your negative thoughts, you are on the path towards the law of attraction.

Phew. We got all of the negative stuff out of the way.

Now, let's focus on the positives.

Focus on Your Frequency

The next step on the path towards the law of attraction is raising your frequency. Your frequency is your energy level, and we understand objects based on their wavelengths. Everything has a frequency. The color red has a distinctly different frequency than the color blue. A squirrel squeak is a higher frequency than a whale song. We understand every color, sound, and being in the universe because of the wavelengths it projects.

We are energy. We consume it and emit it on physical and metaphysical levels. The law of energy states that "nothing in this universe was created or destroyed."

This means that since the Big Bang, all matter has been the same. None has been added, and none has been taken away. It has all been recycled, repurposed, and shown itself in different forms. Neil Degrasse Tyson says that since we are all made up of the same material from the Big Bang, we are biologically connected to everything else that has lived and is living.

We are part of an interconnected web between us and every other creature living. We receive and exchange energy with all other objects in the universe. Therefore, the power of the universe picks up on the energy we emit, which expresses itself as thoughts. It knows when our thoughts are negative and are blocked. It responds under it. The universe has no control over your destiny, but it returns the energy that you put out. Your energy is what you have complete control over. The universe mirrors our frequency.

Your negative thoughts like stress, frustration, anxiety, and depression will lower our frequencies. With that logic, the universe responds when we are at a higher frequency. That is when we can take control of our thoughts and mitigate the negative ones. Remember, negative thoughts will always be there; what matters is how you handle them. Once you raise your frequency, you will be on a clearer pathway to attract your deepest desires.

How to Raise Your Vibration

The first step is to have a compassionate handle on your thoughts. Once you are in the habit of stopping your negative thoughts and buffering them with positive affirmations, you can take the next few steps to raise your frequency.

Meditation

Meditation is an opportunity for you to set aside intentional time to only think about positive affirmations. It's best to meditate in the early morning when the world is waking up as well. After a good night's rest, your energy is freshest in the morning. You must channel it effectively. Starting in the morning will start your day on the right foot. If you wake up and start checking Snapchat, that will mess with your frequencies and focus. Through morning meditation, you can reinforce the good feelings you are trying to cultivate and make them a daily practice.

Drink Water

Water helps purify the body and soul. Being hydrated is one of the most important ways to take care of our bodies because it IS our bodies. Water makes up 76% of our brain and 84% of our blood.

Science has shown that we can go nearly a month without eating and still be able to function (I wouldn't recommend weight lifting or climbing a mountain if this happens, but you get the point). However, we can only last a WEEK without water. Water is vital to our being (vital and water both share the same root word).

Water cleanses you. Water flushes out toxins that we absorb through our environments as well. Be sure to drink 8-10 glasses of water a day and have some water every half an hour. Keep a water bottle close to you at all times. If you find that it's hard to remember to drink water, set a timer on your phone. That way the cleansing process is always happening.

Eat Hi-Vibe Food

As stated before, we are all connected to every other object in the universe. That applies to our food as well. Food has frequencies in the same way animals and colors do. Whole foods like fruits, vegetables, grains, beans, nuts, and seeds have high frequencies. Guess the wavelength of a Cheeto?

Whole foods that are organic and ethical have the highest frequencies. When we eat hi-vibe food, we raise our own frequencies and make them stronger from the inside out.

Breathe

Taking deep breaths will help us check in with ourselves. Our brains are connected to our breath. When we are stressed, we take short sporadic breaths that continue to stress us out. When we take deep, long breaths, it generates a sense of calmness throughout our whole bodies. It reminds you to take it easy and slow down. We are replenished on a cellular level when we inhale. An easy breathing technique to start with is to count your breath. Find a comfortable place to sit and inhale for four counts. Then hold your breath for four counts and exhale for eight. Do this cycle for five-ten minutes and notice how centered you feel after.

Get Enough Rest

Sleep is imperative to our overall well being. Our circadian rhythms regulate our hormones. When we don't get enough sleep, mental health issues like anxiety and depression become harder to control. Sleep regulates our stress levels, cleans out toxins from the day, and gives us the energy to have a productive day. When we have our solid, uninterrupted eight hours of sleep, we wake up with a raised frequency.

Get Moving

Movement is a necessary asset to vibrations. A string only plays music when it is plucked! The more you move, the higher your vibrations are. Now that doesn't mean run on a treadmill for 2 hours straight and then swim across the ocean. Everyone enjoys different kinds of exercises. Experiment and find yours. That could be joining a local soccer team, lifting weights, or attending a weekly yoga class. Don't do any exercise that you don't feel connected to. Once you feel emotional resistance, that means it's time to find something new. Move your body however feels good for you.

When you are happy and moving, it gets your blood flowing. When we exercise, it naturally releases endorphins and relieves stress. We can work through those negative thoughts that have been building up inside of us and release the tension through movement.

Nature Cleanse

Being in nature heightens your vibe faster than others. Nature has the highest frequency, so bathing yourself in the natural world will help you achieve a higher vibration more quickly. All of the trees, flowers, woodland creatures, rivers, and stones have high frequencies. When you spend too much time in malls or in a car, your frequency is lowered.

When you connect with nature, you are closest to the natural vibrations of the universe. Set an intentional time to put down your phone or computer and look up at the stars, put your feet in the grass, or go for a long walk in the forest. It will show you the oneness you are intertwined in.

If you live in a city, go to a park or fill your house with plants. Invest in a bike or participate with your city's bike-sharing system (nearly every city has one these days). Studies suggest that individuals who have more nature around them are less stressed and happier individuals. Happier individuals mean a higher vibe.

Cleanse Your Social

You don't just want to clear out your body of toxins; we want to clean out the mind as well. We are like sponges and absorb negative energies that other people put out. Watching reality TV, scrolling through Instagram, and clicking through Pinterest into the night is just as bad as eating a box of Chips AHoy and french fries for dinner.

We are surrounded by an overwhelming amount of images and stories that insert negative stories in our heads. They can throw us off course. Now, visualization and images will be important later on, but you need to be in control of what you let in. Even if you can't give up Youtube, maybe just switch to corgi videos instead of makeup tutorials.

Cleansing your social might not just mean deleting specific apps. It might also include certain relationships. Toxic friends or family members might constantly thwart your progress. You will have to assess each relationship in your life and analyze if they are a healthy influence or a draining one. If there are individuals that you can't remove from your life, you can have a conversation with them about their negative attitudes and how it affects you. This conversation can happen in a non-confrontational way. If you don't think the conversation will be helpful in person, then consider sending an email or writing a letter. When you choose to surround yourself with positive people, your frequency will elevate!

Do What You Love

The best way to raise your frequency is to do something that you love. Go to a dance class, brunch with friends, or garden. Whatever it is, make it a priority throughout your day and week. When we prioritize positive activities in our lives, our lives become more positive. By doing what you love, you will emit more positivity and happiness, and what does the universe do when you emit these emotions? It provides you with more positivity and happiness.

Practice Acts of Kindness

There is no denying that practicing acts of kindness raises your frequency exponentially. When you are kind to others, you are passing on positive energy to them. Transferring positive vibes not only benefits the receiver but becomes a ripple effect. You inspire other people to become kind to other strangers or loved ones.

You can practice an act of kindness with any relationship. Bring your mom flowers, tell your partner how grateful you are for them, pay for the coffee of the stranger behind you. Every act of kindness increases your frequency. However, your motivation can't be because you want to raise your frequency: it has to be genuine (WakingTimes, 2016).

Chapter 2:
Visualize, Act, and Be Grateful

Visualization

Now that you are in full alignment and you feel higher frequencies coursing through your body, it's time to visualize your desires.

The law of attraction doesn't work if you are just sitting and hoping that something changes. You do need to have your heart's desires in mind, but you can't just passingly think about them: you have to feel them.

Visualization is a crucial component of the law of attraction. You need to visualize your desires unfolding in your imagination but feel like it is actually happening. What does it feel like to be on stage in front of 1000 people? Or watch your daughter be born? Or finally, finish your book?

Scientists have done studies on the brain in action vs. visualization. The same areas of our brains light up whether or not we are actually experiencing something. That means that our brain believes we are doing a specific action or experiencing a certain event even when we are lying in a CAT scan.

So when you are visualizing your dreams, you have to make sure it is feelings based. You aren't a viewer peering in from a window. You are actively feeling the same emotions of your vision as if it is happening. If you are climbing the top of Mt. Kilimanjaro, you feel the air on your face and sun on your skin. If you are performing for a huge music venue, you see the crowd shouting out at you and feel the adrenaline in your body. You need to feel what it is like to be there. Give your visualization details: the more specific, the better. Your mind will believe it is happening and send out those brainwaves to the universe that it is happening, which will make it happen.

Nurture your vision like a plant and watch it grow inside of you.

Act in Accordance

An imperative point about the law of attraction is that you must act on it. What you desire is manifested through the combination of positive thoughts and positive action. If you want a new job, you can't just keep going to the same job and hope that something will change. You need to update your Linkedin, apply to new jobs, and tell other people that you are interested in a different position. You HAVE to act.

Once you have your goal in mind and are putting positive affirmations around that goal, every decision you make must be around fulfilling that goal. Each choice you make throughout your day must be mentally checked and approved by your goal. If you want a new job, don't spend your weekend playing video games. Go to networking events, get after hour drinks with co-workers, or go to job fairs. You shouldn't deny yourself a full life, but the more in alignment your actions are to your goal, the faster it will come.

Don't Worry about the How

A mental block that comes up for a lot of people is how.

I have these grand dreams and visualizations, but how are they going to happen?

You don't need to worry about how it is going to happen. How am I going to find my soulmate? How am I going to get my dream job? How will I find the funds for a new car? As long as you continue to visualize your dreams in vivid detail and emit powerful and positive brain waves, the universe will respond in accordance.

But you do need to stay focused and in alignment with your visualizations. Once you have a crystal clear vision, every action you do needs to be in alignment with that vision. If you are trying to get fit, you can't sit and watch 4 hours of Netflix while eating a box of ice cream sandwiches. You have to sign up for a gym membership, put your phone down, and lift some weights. You have to meal plan and avoid unhealthy foods. You need focused attention on what you are doing and eliminate distractions or anything that will throw you off course. If an action isn't in alignment with your vision, you have to avoid it. As you become in alignment with your vision, it will happen faster.

Gratitude

The most significant component that guarantees the law of attraction works is practicing gratitude. Be grateful for what you already have—being able-bodied, having a home, having a job, and a family. Even if you are dissatisfied with what you have, expressing gratitude is the most reliable way to manifest your desires and possibly supercharge them.

Expressing gratitude towards the tiniest things—having long fingernails, getting a free coffee, having an easy commute—will accelerate your manifestations. Gratitude is imperative, especially on the hardest days. The days where you feel like the world is against you. When you start to see the positives within that day, you will begin to see that each day is filled with magical blessings and opportunities. Each day you are alive, regardless of what state, is a day to be joyful.

If you ever feel entitled to a manifestation, you are not practicing gratitude correctly. Entitlement blocks manifestations from happening because it is negative energy. It blocks you from seeing what you already have and should feel grateful for having. You can't gain more when you are noticing all that you don't have. The universe doesn't discriminate against energy, so if you are thinking about what you don't have—I don't have a new car, I don't have a hot body, I don't have my soulmate—the universe will not supply it to you. A fundamental principle of the law of attraction is that you create your reality through your thoughts. So if your mind is fixated on what you don't have and you are angry about what you SHOULD have, the universe will continue to manifest blocks. The only way that the universe will manifest what you desire is by expressing gratitude for what you already have and what comes to you. When you begin to be grateful for the smallest parts of your day, entitlement should melt away. *"If the only prayer you said in your whole life was ' thank you' that would suffice." –* Meister Eckhart

Gratitude Exercises

Say thank you once you wake up.

Say thank you as you brush your teeth.

Say thank you every time something lovely happens throughout your day.

Say thank you when the sun shines, when you see a sunset or a gorgeous cloud.

(Hurst, 2019)

Morning gratitude meditation: Meditate on the constants in your life that make you grateful: happy and healthy friends and family, a lovely home, a stable income, a loyal partner, a cozy cat. Practice general gratitude every morning to help you see how much you already have throughout your day.

Nature gratitude: Express a moment of gratitude when you interact with nature. Nature settings are filled with higher frequencies, which will positively impact your frequency. Take moments of gratitude for the natural beauty this world is overflowing with: the garden on your block, your house plants, or walks through the woods.

Now Gratitude: Pause at random moments throughout your day and take a moment of gratitude. Check-in with how your day has been going and be grateful for what has happened so far. If something unpleasant has happened, see what it can teach you, and how can you realign your day to become more pleasant. Set a reminder on your phone 4-5 times a day to pause and say thanks.

Speak Gratitude: Tell someone in your life you are grateful for them and why. This unexpected act of kindness will raise your vibration and positively impact that person's day as well. You will also be planting a seed in that person to express gratitude in their life.

Evening Gratitude Meditation: Close your night out the way that you began it. Either journal or meditate on the beautiful things that happened during your day. The smallest thing counts. Maybe you got a good parking spot at work; you had a great conversation with your sister, or you got to make the cashier at the grocery store laugh. Add up all of the little things you are grateful for and recognize how abundant your day was.

Gratitude Journal: Take a journal and write out what you are grateful for each day. As you write, feel the love inside of you and put that love into each word you write. You can journal right when you wake up or as you go to bed. Gratitude is not only the secret ingredient to optimal manifestation: it maximizes it.

Now that you are raising your frequencies, visualizing vividly, expressing gratitude, and aligning your actions with your vision, we can begin focusing on how to attract the grandest life.

Chapter 3:
Wealth Mindset

Napoleon Hill is synonymous with money manifestation. He is the author of one of the original and most popular books on money manifestation, *Think and Grow Rich*! Although he is the godfather of mental wealth, he started from humble beginnings. He was born in 1883, on the cusp of the Civil War. He and his parents squeezed themselves into a one-room log cabin in the deep Appalachian woods. When he was nine, his mother passed away, which left a gaping wound in his heart. He then began to act out and was thought of as a wild child in his town. Then, his father got remarried to Martha. Unlike the traditional stepmother story, Martha was a significant influence on Hill and his development. She saw something in him that not even his biological parents could. Martha began taking Hill to church and had him swap out his gun for a typewriter.

"If you become as good with a typewriter as you are with that gun, you may become rich and famous and known throughout the world," she told him. Hill swiftly made the switch and dedicated himself to writing. His actions started getting him in alignment with his true calling. Within five years, he was working at a local newspaper and then the popular *Bob Taylor's Magazine*. This popular magazine focused on wealth and power advice, planting the seeds of prosperity in Hill's subconscious. His first assignment was to interview the wealthiest man in America of his time: Andrew Carnegie. During that interview, Carnegie planted a seed in Hill's mind. Carnegie told the young writer that there needs to be a book on "the philosophy of success." Carnegie had noticed that people continue to make the same mistakes, but a few key elements could prevent younger generations from having to go through a trial and error process.

Everything people would need for success would be bound together in one book. Hill was the man to write it. Carnegie then introduced Hill to all of his successful friends. That serendipitous meeting jump-started a 20-year long project where Hill interviewed the most successful men in America. Hill sat down with the financial juggernauts of the time: Theodore Roosevelt, Thomas Edison, John D. Rockefeller, Henry Ford, and Alexander Graham Bell, to name a few. In the book, Hill writes out the common denominators that all of these successful and wealthy influencers share. These individuals all share the same tenement philosophies of the law of attraction.

The underlying messages in Hill's book are a 1930s translation of the law of attraction fundamentals.

Hill discovered the steps to bringing about your desires: visualize them and act on them with positive energy. All of the individuals interviewed stated that they were masters of their own futures. When you are focused on a goal, and exclusively on that goal, the universe gets out of your way. Your mindset must be positive. You cannot have negative thoughts like hatred, jealousy, or selfishness harboring within you. Positive attitudes bring real successes. The mind is limitless. We set our own limitations. Each human is made up of their dominating thoughts. Each person has control over what they think.

The subconscious mind responds to all thoughts, positive or negative. Repetition of positive thoughts will strengthen one's faith. You must visualize riches to see them in your bank account. Your subconscious responds to your thoughts and emotions. It doesn't distinguish between positive and negative. *"There are no limitations to the mind except those we acknowledge. Both poverty and riches are the offspring of thought."*- Napoleon Hill.

Sound familiar? *Think and Grow Rich!* was published in 1937 towards the tail end of the Depression. But people didn't know that the end of the depression was near at the time. Nearly 20% of Americans were unemployed when this book was published. After almost eight years of being in an economic downturn, it must have been hard even to imagine times getting better. However, the book flew off the shelves so fast that it needed to be reprinted within the first three weeks of being sold. This was at a time when people were living on rations and counting their pennies. What happened after the selling of this book? America got called into action and pulled itself out of the Depression, which was followed by the most substantial economic boom of the century. One can't link causality, but it sure is a convenient coincidence that the American Dream was reimagined after the publication of this book. *Think and Grow Rich!* is still being read by the newest generations and has sold close to 30 million copies around the globe.

Redefine Money Relationships

One of the aspects that Hill recognizes immediately is limiting beliefs around money. Hill understood that becoming rich starts with dismantling the notion that you can't have wealth. Most of us believe that we won't make more than our parents or rise above the social class we were born into. We learn a lot of our limiting beliefs from our family, friends, coworkers, and teachers. They have stayed stagnant with their mentality, which is why they probably haven't seen much change in their bank account. Sure, they may be financially stable, but are they thriving? Do they have enough for a boat? A lake house? An annual trip to Europe? Can they afford their dreams right now? Those who have limiting beliefs about money won't see a drastic change in their bank accounts. We have picked up these beliefs from a young age, and they tenaciously hold down positive ideas around money.

A large area around money is debt. If you are in massive amounts of debt right now, anxious thoughts around debt will continue to keep you there. The bills need to be paid, the collectors are calling, and you are getting eviction notices on your apartment. Your debt is keeping you up at night and not letting you have a good rest. You believe that money is hard to come by, and you need to put in long hours to make a dent in your debt.

Whatever your financial situation, know that your negative thoughts might have manifested you there. Remember that the universe responds to all thoughts, positive or negative. So if you are focused on debt, believe that you can't afford your favorite items, or find the world to be too expensive, it will be. But flipping the script can lead you to a life of abundance.

Money is not a bad thing to desire. Money provides us with security, new opportunities, and a chance to live a more abundant life. Money is necessary to be safe and sane. Having money alleviates stress and gives you mental freedom.

Here are some common limiting beliefs that might be swimming in your subconscious.

"Money is the root of all evil."

Money is not the root of all evil. More corrupt actions typically happen out of poverty. Yes, rich people can be corrupt, but poverty pushes people toward crimes much more and faster than wealth does.

"Money is hard to come by."

If you believe money is hard to acquire, it will be. When we put up mental walls around goals, the walls become taller and harder to climb. When we release those mental blocks, we notice the door that opens us into a room of abundance.

"Money can't buy you happiness."

No, money can't buy you happiness, but those who are financially secure are happier in comparison to those who are in poverty. Also, you know what makes people happy? Ice cream. How do you get ice cream? With money.

"Money isn't everything."

Money isn't everything, but having money means you can invest more in your friends and family. You can donate to charities, give back to your community, or give your loved ones the best holiday season. You can use your money to give someone else everything.

"You don't deserve to be rich/have money."

Who deserves anything? We are all positioned to live our most luxurious lives possible. We deserve what we desire and work for.

"You can't have wealth."

Thinking you can't have wealth could have been thoroughly seeded from your childhood. Notice who started saying these ideas to you and then compare it to the type of person they are. Chances are, they probably weren't wealthy themselves. They were projecting their life experiences onto you and anticipating the same would happen. The only person who has control of your destiny is you.

"You aren't meant to be wealthy."

"Meant to" is defined by you and you alone. Your destiny can be whatever you want it to be. Whatever you set your mind to will be meant to be.

"I will have more problems if I have too much money."

The problems that arise from having too much money won't nearly be as detrimental as bankruptcy, psychological stress, an inability to pay your bills or losing your housing. Those are real problems. Once you have enough money, you will be able to put your current issues in perspective.

"If I have too much money, people will stop being my friends."

Once you have enough money to provide for yourself and your family, it would be gracious to treat your friends to dinner or gifts. You will also see who your real friends are once your financial situation is lusher. This could help you discern who is a true friend and who is an opportunist.

"Rich people are evil."

Are Bill and Melinda Gates evil? Is Oprah evil? Wealthy people have always been paying it forward, hence the word philanthropy.

"Money is a limited resource."

We can print more money. Like air, there is more than enough to go around. You just need to find your path, and you will be overflowing with riches.

Once you dismantle these limiting beliefs and begin acting in alignment with your values, you will start to see your bank account flourish like fertilized flowers.

Create Positive Mindsets

Now that you have begun to unsew your negative money beliefs, you can begin to reupholster your mindset. There is a multi-step process that you can walk through to start manifesting the money and abundance that you want in your life. That begins with intention.

It should be a simple intention. No novels here.

You can write out intentions that make sense to you and feel realistic, but it's good to go big. The universe rewards the bold. In an ideal world, how much money would you like to manifest, and within what time frame? Do you want another $1000 in a month? $10,000 in the next six months? Write out a specific timeline and amount for your goals. The more precise, the better. That way, you are giving yourself a tunnel to focus down. It's harder to get off track when you are only going down one.

Once you have your target goal in mind, you want to begin to prime your mind. That means setting up space for you to be reminded of your goal in as many places in your environment as possible. That could be wearing your fanciest clothing or jewelry while practicing your affirmations, or creating a vision board of what you would do with that money. A fancy house. The model car you want. A new wardrobe. Having visions of it around your space will help keep your mind primed for what you want and keeping it in your consciousness. This priming will then bleed into your subconscious mind and help you manifest your desires faster.

The next step is to feel as though the money has already manifested itself. While you are manifesting, you have to feel what it is like to see $100,000 in your bank account or what it feels like to drive around in your new Tesla. A huge part of the law of attraction is feeling as though you have already attracted what you want. The universe will respond to these feelings of focused positivity as if you have already attracted your desires. It will then step out of your way to attract more of it. Remember, the brain can't distinguish between reality and your imagination. The more you physically embody your desires, the more your subconscious will call out to the universe to manifest it for you.

The next step is to love the money that you already have. Remind yourself that you are already more wealthy than you could ever imagine. If you get upset every time you see a bill or think about your debt, your mindset is putting that energy out into the universe. The universe can't distinguish between positive or negative energy; it responds to the energy you are emitting. When you get upset, it blocks your prosperity flow. So love whatever money you do have and express gratitude for it. Expressing gratitude for the money that you already have, even if it is just four dollars in your bank account, will heighten your frequency and clear the channel for you to receive more.

Lastly, you will need to remember to take it one day at a time. The more you practice manifestation, the easier it becomes. However, in the beginning, it can take a while to clear out your deeply embedded negative mindsets around money. The constant cleansing process of money blockages and replacing them with affirmations will be the most rewarding journey you go down. If you get frustrated, the universe will respond to that with more debt and block the money that could have been flowing to you. You need to practice patience and be gentle until the blocks are completely cleared. A full cleansing could take a different amount of time, depending on how dedicated you are to the process.

Mantras, Meditations, and Exercises

Now that we have cleared limiting beliefs around money and set up a ritual around affirmations, it's time to recite some. Remember that the world is made up of energy. Both you and and money are forms of energy. You must become in sync with that energy for it to come to you. Aligning positive thoughts around money will only foster more money. Following are some exercises you can write out or recite to yourself.

I love money because...

I love money because it funds my passions.

I love money because I can do more with money for others than I can when I'm poor.

I love money because it gives me the life I want to live.

I love money because I am secure and can move through any financially tough situation.

I love money because I can share my wealth more the more of it I have.

I love money because I can travel more with it and meet more wonderful people.

I love money because it helps me to provide for my family, and we can live more securely and do more family activities with it.

I love money because I can live a richer life with it.

Attraction Affirmations

Money flows to me effortlessly.

My income is always increasing.

Money is good for my well being.

Every day, I attract more money.

I am open to the abundance of money around me.

Money is easy to get and easy to receive.

The amount of money I can attract is limitless.

I will always have the amount of money that I need.

I attract money every day.

I am a magnet for money.

Opportunities arise for me constantly.

Envisioning you already have it

I have more than enough money.

I have more money than I know what to do with.

I am wealthy.

I am richer than I could ever have imagined in my wildest dreams.

My life is filled with riches.

I am successful and overflowing with abundance.

Envision

While you are writing it out or reciting it to yourself, you have to envision it. The visualization can last for 5-20 minutes of focused concentration. Find a private space to write or meditate without distractions. Visualize seeing $100,000 in your bank account. Feel what it's like to walk around in your new house. Smell the huge garden you have on your acre of land. Whatever your vision is, feel what it is like to already have it.

Make it Happen

The last step is making sure that all of your actions are in alignment with your goal. You can't dream about a new home and then sit in your sad apartment and zone out on Youtube videos for four hours. You have to go out and achieve it. Instead of going out and drinking away your paycheck, put some of it away for your dream. Get an online gig or see if you are up for a promotion. As long as your actions are in alignment with your goals, money manifestation will become an effortless process.

Chapter 4:
Health Mindset

Morris E. Goodman stumbled into a local bookstore on an unsuspecting hot July day in 1970. This recent college dropout was looking for purpose and something to read. He aimlessly perused the books looking for a sign. His slow pace brought him through the quiet asiles until a book had caught his eye.

He paused. His hand reached up and grabbed *Think and Grow Rich!*. Goodman quickly finished the book a few days later and got on the straight and narrow. He started a career in insurance sales. Then in less than a year, he was part of the highest community of insurance salesman: the Million Dollar Round Table. Within a decade, he had started his own successful business, Morris Goodman and Associates. All of this was fueled by what he learned in *Think and Grow Rich!*.

His ambitions continued to reach for the sky. In 1981, he got his pilot's license and was able to afford his own private airplane. On a typical March morning, Goodman decided to go for a ride over the Chesapeake Bay. After a few minutes in the air, without warning, the engine lost power. Goodman had to think quick and tried making an emergency landing at a nearby airstrip in Virginia. As he sped towards land, his plane dove into power lines and caused him to crash. The plane flipped and destroyed not only the aircraft but Goodman's cervical vertebrae, which paralyzed him. When he awoke in the hospital, he was unable to breathe, talk, or swallow without medical assistance. He was told he would never walk again. The only movement and resourceful form of communication he was left with was blinking.

From his account, he knew that he couldn't let what the doctors said dictate his life. He knew that if he stewed in a negative mentality, he would never regain strength and mobility. He made an internal commitment that he would walk himself out of the hospital one day. He gave himself a deadline: Christmas. With his positive mentality and physical therapy, he slowly regained the ability to breathe without a machine. The next step was to be able to speak again, which he did within a few months. Over the summer and fall, he was able to chew, swallow, and eat. Walking was the last challenge. Then on November 13th, 1981, Goodman walked himself out of the hospital entirely on his own. He accomplished this a month earlier than his personal deadline and nine months after the accident. Goodman claims that the tenements of the law of attraction, such as positive mental attitude and determination, were the only thing that prevented him from living a life attached to a machine.

Physical Health

Unfortunately, we don't choose the body that we are born with. We don't choose our height or our shoe size, and our eating habits are often taught to us. Nevertheless, our thoughts help us gain control of our relationship with our bodies. The more we believe in the stories that we are lethargic, overweight, or sick, the more we continue to be so. We have the power to let pain into our body or regain health.

Mind Over Body

The placebo effect is a widely recognized phenomenon in the science community. When scientists organize pill studies to see the impact of certain medications, they will typically implement a control group, a.k.a a placebo group. One group with a particular medical condition is split into two. One group will take the actual medication, and the other will take a sugar pill. Only the scientists know which people are taking the real drug. However, all of the people in the study believe they are taking the actual medication. Those who are taking the sugar pill sometimes see significant improvements, even though they aren't taking the drug. But they BELIEVE they are taking medicine and think that the medication is working for them. The mind convinces itself that it is being healed and that the individual is becoming healthier. Due to the placebo effect, many individuals are eventually cured without taking actual medication. All they are doing is believing that they are becoming healthier.

That doesn't discredit Western medication. Your actions have to be in alignment with your intention. So if you aspire to lose weight, then your actions have to reflect your goal. You have to meal plan, work out, and get to sleep on time. You can't wish you were skinnier, then eat cake and watch James Bond movies until 4 am. So, part of your healing process might be getting surgery, going to a therapist, or taking pills. These actions are part of the process, as well.

Redefining Health Relationships

The first step to bringing about health through the law of attraction is by eliminating stress. Stress will not only block positive healing energies, but it will send negative energy out into the universe and usually worsen your pre-existing health issues. If you have been sick for a long time, that might, ironically, be in a place of comfort. You are so used to being sick that you actually can't see any other way of being. You have to uproot the limiting beliefs around your health. These thoughts might be much more internally created rather than externally created, like limiting beliefs around money. But still, we are the stories we tell ourselves. So the story that you are a sick person or a lazy person or a fat person will only continue to be so. Rewriting those scripts is absolutely in your power. Here are some limiting beliefs around health.

On Sickness

I've never been healthy and probably never will.

I get sick so quickly.

Stress rules my life.

I'll never feel well again.

I have always lived with pain.

I may never recover.

It is going to take a long time to recover.

I'm going to get sick; I can feel it.

How to Debunk

When you have limiting beliefs around your health, that only fosters more stress and anxious thoughts. These thoughts will suppress not only your immune system, but they will also block positive healing energies from coming in. If you don't believe you can be healthy, you never will be. If you turn off those thoughts and focus on healing and positive affirmations, the healing process speeds itself up. Most of us are born healthy, and sickness is, hopefully, a short window of time. As long as you allow it to be temporary.

On Losing Weight

Exercising is too hard.

I hate exercising.

I'm not an exerciser.

Healthy food is boring.

Healthy food doesn't taste good.

Losing weight is uncomfortable and painful.

Diets don't work for me.

I can never eat cake again.

How to Debunk

Our society sadly values skinniness and fit bodies over curvier folks. These stories are especially targeted towards women who are told specific skinny focused messages about their bodies from an early age. Girls as early as age six sometimes believe they need to lose weight; although, they don't understand what that means. Their male counterparts don't embody these messages (Hurst, 2019).

Many people feel shame around their weight, regardless of whether they are in a safe weight range or not. Guilt around our guts will only push people down a spiral of fat-shaming thoughts. When you think "fat" thoughts, it will be harder for you to lose the weight you so wish you didn't have. Stress makes it harder for us to think clearly, and interestingly enough helps store fat. Emotional eating comes from stress and not being mindful of your eating habits.

Think about how much your body does for you. It carries you from point A to point B. It allows you to experience so much of the world. It is perfect exactly as it is. Once you accept your body as perfect, it becomes much easier to love.

On Fatigue

I'll never get better.

I'm always going to feel tired.

I'm not a good sleeper.

I'm just a tired person. I never feel fully rested.

How to Debunk

If you complain you are always tired, you will always feel tired. Tiredness is a state of being, as is having the energy to go for a run. Begin to analyze why you might be feeling tired. Are you going to bed at 3 am every night? Are you working too many jobs? Is stress making it hard for you to sleep? The first step is to analyze your sleep patterns and see if there are any daily practices you might be doing, intentionally or not, that is thwarting good sleep. Keep a daily journal to track yourself. Write down what you eat, the last time you had caffeine, and when your last meal was. Write down when you go to bed, wake up, and at how many times throughout the night you wake up and for what reason. At the end of the week, see what you are doing or feeling that might inhibit a good night's rest.

Create a Positive Mindset

Just like the money manifestation, you have to take the same steps to visualization and action. Now that you have targeted what your limiting beliefs are around your health, you can begin the healing process, mentally at least. If you follow these steps consistently, you will start to feel healthier and live the active life you deserve. Again, that all begins with intention.

Since health manifestations are a little more specific, take your limiting belief, and reverse it. Instead of thinking, "I'm unhealthy," think, " I'm the healthiest I've ever been!" It's necessary to be as specific as possible. If you have pain in your arm, start there. If you are looking for overall well-being, craft a holistic mantra. Find your intention and stick to it.

The next step is to create a positive, healing space. Look at your home, office, or car, and notice if it is cluttered. Having a clean and manageable space will allow your mind to relax and focus on healing. Spaces affect how we feel, and one that has stressful vibes will enhance your stress. This also goes for your kitchen cabinets. Sugar, alcohol, processed foods, and sometimes caffeine can prevent you from having a healthy lifestyle and, in conjunction, mindset. Target what specific foods are bogging you down and eliminate them from your kitchen. When you are going grocery shopping, don't walk down the aisle where these unhealthy items are passively placed. If you avoid passing them by, you will be less tempted to purchase them. Eliminate them from your routine. When you are going out to restaurants, tell your eating companions about your dedication to eating healthy. If they want burgers, find a place that has good burgers and salads. You need to begin to create an environment that serves your healthy lifestyle.

If you are looking to get fit, create a vision board or Pinterest board of what you want to look like. Put it in a few places around your home to remind yourself what you are aiming for. That will keep your mind primed for that goal and help keep you on track.

The next step is to feel as though you already have the body or health that you want. When you are meditating or writing, you have to emulate the feeling of being energized, healthy, thin, or not in pain. You need to feel as though you have already become the person you want to be. Remember, the universe responds to energy, so if you are putting out positive energy of health and fitness, the universe will keep you on track.

After feeling health radiate through you, you need to practice loving your body. You need to love that you are healthy, fit, and sexy. Loving your body will also alleviate the stress that has been embedded in your psyche. If you look in the mirror and are still disappointed with how you look, the universe will hear that. If you get frustrated through this process, the universe will plateau your health. It will respond accordingly and block any healthy, positive energy that was flowing towards you. Love your body, and it will love you back.

Similar to the money manifestation, healing manifestation is a process. But don't get discouraged. Your cells change every day, every second of every day. Therefore, every second is an opportunity to be healthy and make good choices around your health. You don't want to lift 100 pounds on your first day of exercising. You need to work yourself up to that gradually. The more you practice positive, healthy mindsets, the stronger you will become. Be gentle with yourself on the days where you weren't motivated to work out or were too tired to get out of bed. Recenter yourself when things don't go accordingly, and promise to do better ASAP. If you get off track, the best thing to do is get right back on that horse instead of waiting until "tomorrow." Tomorrow will bleed into next week and then a month from now and then never. Remind yourself of your intention and stick to it.

Positive Affirmations

Now your health is prioritized. Check.

You know exactly how you want to be healthy. Check.

And you have removed the limiting blocks that you had around your health. Check.

It is time to write out or meditate around affirmations. Remember that the world is made up of energy. You emit energy, and you take in energy. Your cells are energy, vibrating inside of you as you read. When you treasure your cells, they will return the favor. Here are mantras and meditations you can write out or recite to yourself.

On Bodies

My body is perfect.

I love my body.

My body does so much for me.

My body is beautiful.

My body is strong.

On Health

I have always been healthy.

I am going to be healthy in no time.

Health is my priority.

I love having a healthy lifestyle.

Being healthy comes easily to me.

I love being healthy and strong for my family and friends.

I'm so grateful for being able to be healthy all the time.

I am in perfect health.

I have never felt healthier.

I have never been this strong.

I am getting stronger every day.

Strength is an unlimited resource.

On Sleep

I love sleeping.

I love feeling well-rested.

I love getting to bed on time.

I feel great every morning.

Envision

You have to envision yourself at your healthiest state while you are writing or meditating. The visualization can last for 5-20 minutes with deep concentration. Find a private space to write or meditate without distractions. Envision your ideal body and feel it on a cellular level. See yourself doing a backflip, enjoy the endorphin rush of finishing a marathon, or the beauty of not being in pain as you go for a walk. Whatever your vision is, feel it in your body down to the nucleus.

Make it Happen

The last step is making sure that all of your actions are in alignment with your goal. You can't think about being fit and go party all night, get drunk, order cheesy fries and pizza at 3 am and get to bed at 8 am. Every action you take must be in alignment with your desires. If you want to lose weight, get a gym membership or an accountability buddy, begin tracking your calories, and clear out your kitchen (and your snack corner in your bedroom) of Poptarts. When your actions are in alignment with your goals, you will be in control of your health instead of it being in control of you.

Be Grateful

Gratitude is the keystone to manifestation success. If you feel entitled to a healthy body but aren't working towards it, it won't happen. You must ground yourself in gratitude for what you already have. Be grateful you can read this sentence. Be grateful you can hear your roommates bicker. Be grateful you can run, bike, or hike a mountain whenever you feel like it. The smallest feelings of gratitude will do wonders. The more grateful you feel, the higher your vibrations will be, and the faster your health will return to you.

Chapter 5:
Success, Happiness, and Love

In 1956, Oprah Winfrey was born into extreme poverty. It was so severe, her grandmother would repurpose potato sacks for Oprah to wear to school. Oprah was born to an unwed black woman in rural Mississippi. Her life began two years after Brown vs. Board of Education. It was a ruling that knocked down the pernicious Jim Crow laws that had implicitly dictated southern laws since the end of the Civil War. Women had only had the right to vote for less than 40 years and were still disincentivize to participate in politics or receive an education. Needless to say, little Oprah Winfrey was born into an unwelcoming world.

Oprah's mother eventually relocated them to Milwaukee, where Oprah was molested as a child. She ran away and became pregnant at 14, a time when most girls are concerned with acne on their face. She gave birth to her son before her term was finished, and her son died shortly after. She was given another chance. A twist of fate sent her off to live with her father in Tennessee, who prioritized her education. She wasn't going to take this new life lightly. While still in high school, she managed to land a radio job, which kicked down an auspicious domino effect. Once she graduated, she had managed to move from radio to television and began her television career as a co-anchor for Nashville's WLAC-TV local evening news. She was not only the youngest person on the air, but also the first black female to ever be an anchor on Nashville's news station. Having a black woman on the air when coals of Jim Crow were still smoldering was an astounding feat.

Her passionate readings on the news caught the eye of many producers and news watchers. Within a few years, she had ping-ponged her way from Nashville to Baltimore to Chicago. Within a decade, she was recognized as the best TV news anchor in Chicago, beating out Phil Donahue, the "king of daytime television." How a black, curvy woman was able to rise to the top of an all-white, male industry is still inspirational to this day. The Oprah Winfrey show lasted for 25 years and was the highest-rated daytime television program in the history of the United States. Oprah Winfrey quickly became a household name. She became the first black female billionaire and is in the top ranks of the most influential woman in the world. She swapped her potato-sack for Versace and has won numerous awards. She is the voice of a generation. Her accolades and ambition continue to wow and inspire us to this day. She is by far one of the most inspirational, successful women in the world, and she owes it to the law of attraction.

Not only is she a master of the law of attraction, but she has also been an amplifier of it.

In an interview with Larry King, Oprah professes that she called her first movie roll into her life. She had become obsessed with the book *The Color Purple* by Alice Walker. She was recommending it to everyone she knew. One unsuspecting day, she got a call from a casting agent for a movie. She asked, what movie? When she came into the studio, she realized she was auditioning for *The Color Purple*. After she left, she didn't hear anything for months. She continued to pray for the agency to call her back. One unsuspecting day, she was tired of asking the universe to bring the movie to her. She told Larry King that she began singing a biblical song about surrendering. Then the phone rang. That phone call was Steven Spielberg asking her to come to California the next day to be in *The Color Purple*. The year that *The Color Purple* was released, she was nominated for an Academy Award for best-supporting actress for her performance as Sophia in the movie. From that moment on, she knew the power of the law of attraction. Her mindset on the power in her life was forever changed (Hurst, 2018).

"It is very true that the way you think creates reality for yourself." - Oprah during a Larry King interview.

Since then, Oprah has been a massive advocate for the law of attraction. She has had Rhonda Byrne, writer of *The Secret*, on The Oprah Winfrey show when the book came out and had a whole panel of individuals toot the horn of the principles of *The Secret*.

Oprah is the pinnacle example of using the law of attraction for happiness and success. One of the reasons it might be so extremely beneficial to her is because she is a philanthropist. She is known as one of the biggest philanthropists in the world.

She has not hoarded her money away like Mr. Scrooge. She has consistently used her money for the benefit, aid, and lifting up of other people. Her success is because she does her work for others rather than herself. The more she gave back, the more her frequency was raised. Her success is a direct response from the universe, which continued to flow in success towards her ("Living the Law of Attraction," n.d.).

Success vs. Happiness

It is also important to note that success and happiness are not synonyms of each other. However, they tend to go hand in hand. You could be perfectly happy sitting under a tree reading and watching a butterfly lie on your finger. Many wouldn't call that success. You could also be giving a speech in front of thousands of people; they scream as you get off stage, and you still feel a void in your heart. That isn't happiness. When the two go together, that is both success and happiness. *"Success is not the key to happiness. Happiness is the key to success. If you love what you are doing, you will be successful."* - Albert Schweitzer

For these manifestations, we will think of success in terms of career and creative achievements and happiness as a state of inner peace. Both will have separate affirmations.

Reframing Success Beliefs

The world is a challenging place. We don't choose what circumstances we are born into. We don't choose our parents, the era, or where in the world we are born. The beginning of our lives is vastly out of our control. It is dictated by our parents, our societal obligations, classroom schedules, and the need for high test scores. We are raised in a world that has a specific definition of success and happiness. People are astonished when individuals take life into their own hands and achieve success in unconventional ways. But these individuals know the secret. They know that their happiness isn't defined by the car they have, by how much money is in the bank, or the fact that they have a beautiful partner. Their success is defined on their own terms, which makes them happy.

Both happiness and success are completely subjective. They are defined by the beholder, not the viewer.

It isn't until we begin to become conscious of the world around us that we can start to see what is in our control: our thoughts.

The first step in achieving happiness and success is to analyze your limiting beliefs. These beliefs are probably implanted in you from an early age. From the television you watched to how your friends and family subliminally talked about success, there are stories that are deeply embedded within us. These beliefs transform into expectations. "I'm only successful if I get into Yale. I'm only successful if I make $100,000 a year. I'm only happy if I have a wonderful partner." The more you believe you aren't worthy of these accomplishments, the harder it will become for you to achieve them.

This is also a tricky area because your external success is quickly judged by others. Your idea of success could be driven by those around you. Maybe you want to impress other people, make your parents proud, or feel like you will never measure up to your older brother. But unless you let go of these limiting beliefs, you will never achieve the happiness you so desperately crave. If you believe the story you tell yourself, you will become it.

These limiting beliefs will hold you back throughout your life. The people who became wildly successful only did so because they believed they could. When you believe in your limitations, it will thwart the abundance of opportunities that come toward you every day. Each morning you wake up is an opportunity to live the best life you couldn't have even dreamed of the night before. If you continue to give power to your limits, then you will only be able to focus on the circumstances of your life. The hardest part is identifying that they even have a hold on you.

Here are some common limiting beliefs around success and how to debunk them.

How you perceive yourself

I'm not worthy of success.

Success never comes to me.

I'm not good enough for that job.

I don't deserve it.

It hurts too much to challenge myself.

I'm comfortable where I am.

Something is wrong with me, which is why I am not happy.

Happiness comes from material things.

I'm too old/young for this.

I'm not smart enough.

I don't know what I'm doing wrong.

I don't have enough experience.

I wasn't born into the right family.

I don't have the right education.

Being honest leads to rejection.

If I relax, all hell will break loose.

Risking being criticized or judged is not worth the pain it could cause.

I'm not important.

I'm inherently unlikable and unlovable.

I'm not self-disciplined.

There's no point in asking for what I want.

No one will support or encourage me.

I'm powerless when it comes to my success.

I can't change how I am.

I'm not strong enough to succeed.

It is scary to be vulnerable.

I can't trust myself.

I'm not smart enough to succeed.

I'm not popular enough for my dreams.

I'm not connected enough.

Others are in my way.

I'm a hopeless mess.

It's selfish if I focus on myself.

How to Debunk

Success is defined on your terms. Your life and accomplishments need to be based on what makes you joyful, what would make you proud, and how you want to be remembered. That all comes from within.

How Others Perceive You

I have to have others' approval to have success.

I care about what X thinks of me.

Other people's opinions matter a lot to me.

I'm nervous about what others will think of me.

I don't want people to judge me.

What I think of myself doesn't matter; it's what others think that does matter.

I feel worthy when I have others' approval.

Everyone else is better than me.

How to Debunk

How others perceive you is a large inhibitor for people who are struggling with success. However, other people's opinions don't matter as much because they are equally as subjective. You can't live your life based on someone else's rules. You have to define your own rules, and success will follow shortly.

Fear of Failure

There is no point in trying.

I'm going to fail anyway.

What if I fail?

I have failed before and will probably fail again.

It's easier to build walls to protect myself.

I am a failure.

It's easier not to try than to fail.

I don't deserve beautiful things/ to be successful.

There's no point in dreaming big. Dreams die anyways.

How to Debunk

Failure is ironically necessary for optimal success. The most successful individuals are those who know what it feels like to fail and know how to bounce back from it. They don't linger in failure. They reframe failure as an opportunity to learn. When you learn from the bumps along your journey, you are more prepared for them in the future. If you are going on a road trip and turn around after the first pothole, you won't be going anywhere. Those who are successful embrace failure because they love learning what they don't know and become stronger from it.

Fear of Success

I can't handle success/happiness.

I don't trust that I can have success/happiness.

I'm just not someone who can complete a job.

I hate having the spotlight on me.

What if people are mean to me because of my success?

What if I can't come through when the time comes?

Success might turn me into someone I'm not.

I'm okay with how things are.

I can't start yet. I'm not ready to begin. I need more time.

I don't have enough time.

I don't have enough energy.

My plate is too full already.

How to Debunk

When fame and glory are so treasured in our society, you would think it would be a contradiction to be afraid of success. However, this is a real fear that holds people back. Remember that success is defined on your terms, not by others' metrics or perceptions. Success takes a lot of work, but the rewards are endless. Every human is entitled to reach for their highest dreams and reap the rewards of their hard work (Novak, 2019).

Here are some common limiting beliefs around happiness and how to debunk them.

Happiness

I don't deserve to have more than I have.

I'm afraid of happiness.

I don't deserve happiness.

Happiness doesn't come naturally to me.

The world is a dark/unfair place.

I have bad luck all the time.

If I get too happy, I'll jinx myself.

Life is hard, and that's just the way it is.

I'll be happy when ___ changes.

Getting my hopes up always leads to disappointment.

I'll never be happy.

I'm selfish if I prioritize my happiness.

My dreams are too big.

My dreams are unrealistic.

How to Debunk

People who claim to be happy all have the same thing in common: they are internally happy. They know that they are in control of whether or not they feel happy or feel successful. These terms are defined on an individual basis. Happiness is an internal state of peace. It means you aren't struggling every day with yourself. You are at emotional homeostasis and are calm and appreciative of every day, regardless of what happens in it.

Create Positive Mindsets

Identifying your limiting beliefs is the first step to overcoming them. Once the light is shined on them, you can begin to brainstorm how to take them down. Happiness and success manifestations take similar steps as the money and health ones, but let's continue to go through them. Like all great journeys, happiness and success begin with intention — neither falls into someone's lap. Happy people intend to be happy. Successful people intend to be successful.

These intentions must be in your voice and feel true to you. You can't put your energy behind an intention you don't believe in or that doesn't call you. Begin by writing out what happiness looks like to you. Is it having a Netflix special? Having your book be published? Is it creating a successful business? Or maybe it is a more straightforward goal, like having a comfortable and lovely home or a happy work environment. Knowing precisely what you want will help you focus on it intensely and prevent you from getting off track.

Once you have set your specific intention, you want to begin to prime your mind. Write out your goal and stick it in places where you will see it often. That way your brain will be seeing it constantly throughout the day. You want your space to reflect the life you want. Turn your intention into your smartphone home page, have it as your computer desktop, or keep it as a post-it note in your bedtime book. Keeping the positive messages around you is a natural way for you to keep your goal at the forefront of your mind.

You can create a vision board of what happiness and success look like to you. Cut out pictures of trips you want to take, tech gadgets you want to buy, or your dream house. Define what happiness and success look like to you and plaster it all over your place.

The next step is to feel that happiness and success have already happened to you. As you write out or meditate your intention, you need to feel it. You need to feel the pen and paper as you sign copies of your newest book. You need to hear the audience as they laugh at your jokes. You need to feel the embrace of a loved one wrap around your body. As you continue to embody the feelings of your success, the universe will pick up on those messages and provide them to you.

After you have felt it, you have to love what you have already been given. You have to love the people that you are already surrounded with. You have to love that your family and friends are happy and healthy. You must love what success you have already achieved and love that your success is limitless. Once the universe recognizes you expressing gratitude for what you already have, it will step out of the way to give you more.

The last piece of the process is patience. Happiness and success goals are marathons, not sprints. You need to take it one day at a time. Each action you take in that day must be in alignment with your greater goal. That is the only way you will be able to achieve it. The more you practice decluttering your brain of limiting beliefs and replacing them with positive affirmations, the stronger your frequency becomes. Some days will feel harder than others. However, with consistent practice, you will feel better once you have positive affirmations in place that buffer you from the hard times. If you struggle with it, adjust your intention. If you feel frustrated or impatient, the universe will pick up on that energy. The universe doesn't discriminate against the type of energy you are putting out. Therefore, negative energy is received just as easily as positive energy. As long as you are kind to yourself during this process, the universe will be kind to you as well.

It's time to find which mantras and meditations are in alignment with your intention. You can journal or recite in your brain the following messages.

Mantras, Meditations, and Exercises

I love myself because...

I love myself because I am worthy of love.

I love myself because I am strong enough to handle any situation.

I love myself because I am successful.

I love myself because I am filled with potential.

I love myself because I am happy.

I love myself because I am in control of my destiny.

Success Affirmations

I am full of abundance.

I am so successful for my age.

I am always attracting success.

Success comes to me naturally.

I am a naturally successful person.

Envisioning You Already Have Success

I see myself landing the job of my dreams.

I see myself smiling and joyful.

I feel filled with energy and enthusiasm.

I see myself waking up every morning elated for the day.

I see myself excited to get to work because I love what I do.

Happiness Affirmations

I deserve to be happy.

I am so proud of myself and what I have accomplished.

I love who I am becoming.

My commitment is to have a happy life.

I am happy.

I'm creating the life I was destined to have.

I work with love to create the life I want.

I am peaceful.

All of my dreams are coming and will come true.

Self-care is not selfish.

I emit radiance.

I choose a life of happiness.

Everyone says how joyful I am.

My happiness makes it easier for others to love me and for me to love others.

I am creating the best version of myself.

I'm not going to give up.

I'm not going to settle.

Happiness is a constant river inside of me.

Each day I am happier than the next.

My happiness is infectious.

I control my happiness.

I choose to be happy.

I live a life of positivity.

I see the glass half full.

I only focus on the positive parts of my day.

Every day is filled with positive moments.

I give myself permission to be happy.

I'm proud that I took one step closer to my dreams today.

There is only one me.

I am a unique human with a positive perspective.

I am valuable.

(Baker, 2017)

Envision

While you are writing out or reciting your intention to yourself, you have to envision it. The visualization can last for 5-20 minutes of intense, focused concentration. Find a private space to write or meditate without distractions. Perfect the vision of seeing your happy family in front of a new home, you shaking the hand of a new client, or you speaking on stage in front of thousands. Feel the smoothness of the doorknob, the firmness of the handshake, and the energy of the theater. Whatever your vision is, feel what it is like to already have it.

Make it Happen

The last step is making sure that all of your actions are in alignment with your goal. You can't dream about your perfect job and scroll through Instagram for an hour. You have to go out and apply for jobs, network, and cold call potential clients. You have to do what you love and work to achieve it. Instead of going out and drinking away your paycheck, put some of it away for your dream. Get an online gig or see if you are up for a promotion. Happiness and success manifestation becomes easy once your actions line up with your desires.

Chapter 6:
Romantic Love

In 2014, Ariana Grande walked into a writer's room for SNL. One of the writers was a new addition to the show, Pete Davison. Neither of them had ever met before. She spent a few hours working with the writers to write sketches for her upcoming appearance on the show. When she finished, her tour manager asked the budding female popstar how the session went. She replied, "I'm going to marry him [Pete]." Ariana Grande wouldn't see Pete Davison for another two years, when she returned to SNL. From there, they started dating. In her album "Sweetener," Ariana Grande writes a 30-second ballad titled Pete Davison that suggests she manifested their love.

"I thought you into my life, woah

Look at my mind, yeah

No better place or a time

Look how they align

Universe must have my back

Fell from the sky into my lap

And I know you know that you're my soulmate and all that."

Although the two had an intense connection, what Ariana didn't realize is that when it comes to love manifestations, we can never manifest a person. We can only manifest a relationship.

Limiting Love Beliefs

Love is possibly one of the largest areas of insecurity, worry, and doubt. It is incredibly personal when we are rejected. It's easy to put up a lot of walls or think we have to change who we are when it comes to pursuing romantic love. On first dates, it's easier to have a mask on than to be your true self. The stakes are so high, yet the rewards are the sweetest.

We exist in a society that values marriage and devalues being single. The story of two people falling in love is the oldest one told. It is in our songs, box office hit movies, best-selling novels, and in nearly every commercial. For many, love is the ultimate goal.

We have been surrounded by limiting beliefs around love since we were children. Maybe you tried holding hands with a classmate, and they ripped their hand out of yours. Maybe you were never noticed by your high school crushes. Or maybe you developed an unhealthy relationship with someone and look negatively at that whole gender now. The limiting beliefs that we create are extremely personal and potent. Maybe you need to forgive a past partner or ask forgiveness from a past relationship before moving forward. Maybe you feel like you have wished for a soulmate for so long that you have lost faith.

The universe is unable to penetrate through the thick walls you build up and won't be able to get to your heart. The longer your heart is shielded from the world, the more it will wither. Here are some general themes and the limiting beliefs around love and how to debunk them.

Dating

Dating is scary.

Dating is hard.

Dating takes too long.

Dating is a waste of time.

What is the point? I'm going to die alone anyway.

Dating is too much energy.

Everyone breaks up anyway, what's the point?

My ideal person isn't out there.

I've got too much going on.

How to Debunk

Dating will always look scary if you think it is scary. People typically want to have nice interactions and aren't going to go on a date to embarrass you. You can take the pressure off of dating by avoiding thoughts of finding "the one." Instead, enjoy the company of the person you are with, regardless of whether you're going on one date with them or end up marrying them. Take expectations away from dating and look at each experience as an opportunity to learn about someone new. Each date holds a lesson within it and will eventually help you become your best self.

Internal Pressure

I'm not worthy of love.

No one will ever love me.

The perfect person isn't out there.

I'm not perfect.

All of the good people are taken.

How to Debunk

You must begin by loving yourself before someone else can love you. No person is able to fill a void inside of you. Only you can do that. Focus on doing the things you love and what makes you loveable. No one will be able to love you if you can't love yourself first. The love that you crave from others must be found inside yourself. No one is perfect, and the idea of perfection is an unrealistic goal. But finding someone who is perfect for you and all of your quirks is realistic and attainable. We need to be our truest selves and love ourselves for who we are before we can even entertain the idea of bringing in another.

External Pressure

The person I love isn't good enough for my parents.

I have to find someone before [specific time].

Letting others get close will lead to pain in the end.

My family will abandon me if I date someone I love.

People won't like the real me.

My friends never like my partners, anyways.

I expect others to hurt me.

How to Debunk

Your life can't be on someone else's timeline or standards. Your parents may not approve of your relationship, but they aren't the ones you have to go home to. Love is love. Putting pressure on yourself or someone else to commit before either of you are ready will push them away and strain the relationship. Let go of external pressure because you can't always choose who you love or know when it will happen. Love comes when you least expect it.

Create Positive Mindsets

The internal work that is needed to unblock your limiting beliefs around love might be the hardest. Our beliefs around love are intertwined with our self-worth and not whether we are talented or beautiful or another superficial construct, but whether we are worthy of love. This might be a painful process because you need to examine yourself and your history with love on the deepest level. This is an area where you could talk it out with friends or a therapist. Once the limiting belief is identified, you can work towards uprooting it and replacing it with positive intentions and affirmations (Cole, 2017).

Your first intention is to love yourself. Unconditionally. You have to love yourself before anyone else can. No one is going to fill the emotional holes inside of you, no matter how wonderful they are. That is work that you must do alone. It is interesting how the world sets us up to doubt ourselves, change who we are, and never feel good enough. But once we love ourselves unconditionally, know how to be gentle with ourselves when we stumble, and how to pick ourselves up again, love flows to us effortlessly.

Once you intend to love yourself, write out why.

I love myself because I am funny.

I love myself because I am kind.

I love myself because I am generous.

I love myself because I am a good listener.

Ground yourself in why you love yourself and intend to be that person even more. You must love yourself in your voice. If it is in someone else's voice, you might not be receptive to it. Your frequency will heighten when you begin to love yourself and act in accordance. Others will see you being your true self and look up to you. You will begin to attract the kinds of people that would be attracted to your truest self. From there, you can take another step towards attracting loving relationships.

Big note: you can't manifest a person. However, you can manifest the type of relationship you want with someone. What are the values you want in that person, and what do you want them to be interested in? Write out what you need in a partner: nature lover, meditates, is an artist, etc. Then write out your deal breakers: can't smoke, can't be an alcoholic, can't be superficial, etc. (Hurst, 2019).

From there, you can begin to draw out what a loving relationship looks like to you. Is it walking through a farmers market together and feeding each other samples of jam? Is it going out to a big game together or skydiving over the Azores? You then need to write out what your ideal relationship looks like. From there, you can manifest it into existence. The more specific you are with your dream, the more direction you give the universe.

Then, just like in the other manifestations, you need to prime your mind. You need to keep visions or affirmations around your home, in your car, or on your phone. That way, your mind is always thinking about it on a subconscious level.

The next order of business is to meditate or write it out and feel like you have already found the love of your life. Feel what it is like to laugh with them, to hold them, to kiss them. Feel what it is like to go to sleep knowing you are dreaming next to the love of your life. See your house together, taking trips with them, and doing what you love together. The universe will align your paths with whom you are destined to be with.

Now you must open your eyes and practice gratitude for the love you already have in your life. Take a moment to say a few words about your closest friends, that funny coworker, or your siblings. Regardless of the relationship dynamic, the relationships you already have are sources of love. These are the people that the universe has brought into your life for a reason. Recognize what they have to teach you, and love them for that. When you feel gratitude for those already in your life, the universe will continue to supply you with loving relationships.

Now begins the patient search for this person. You may not meet them tomorrow, and you will most likely meet them when you least expect it. That may seem contradictory to the law of attraction. But when you practice your manifestations consistently and surrender to the universe, the universe will find the right time to provide you with your soulmate. Those who are in your life are there for a reason, as are the ones who aren't there yet. Your day should be focused on loving yourself and doing what you love. This will naturally heighten your frequency (21 Positive Love Affirmations To Attract Love. n.d.).

Mantras, Meditations, and Exercises

All of my relationships offer a positive, loving experience.

I am worthy of love

I deserve love in abundance.

I love everyone around me.

I love myself.

I love it when others show me love.

I bring loving and caring people into my life.

I'm grateful my partner and I are loving towards each other.

My relationship with my partner is joyful.

I am thankful for all the love in my life.

I am thankful for the universe providing me with my caring partner.

I only have healthy, loving relationships.

I am grateful I have a love of my life.

I love how my partner and I treat each other with respect.

I love giving love.

There is more than enough love to go around.

I love receiving love.

I find love constantly throughout my day.

I am thankful for my partner.

I am grateful for the abundance of loving relationships I have.

My heart is open to receiving love.

I am open to marriage.

I am ready to receive my spouse.

My love grows stronger every day.

I deserve of a long-lasting relationship.

All of my relationships are healthy.

I am constantly surrounded by love.

I am manifesting all the love I need.

I think positively about love.

Each day I bring more love into my life.

My partner is out there.

Envision

You must envision what it feels like to have these positive love affirmations already as you are writing them out or reciting them. The visualization can last for 5-20 minutes of deep focused concentration. Find a private space to write or meditate without distractions. Envision seeing your soulmate for the first time, feel yourself walking down the aisle, or seeing your child being born. Whatever your vision is, see what it is like to already have it.

Make it Happen

The last step is making sure that you are behaving in accordance with your intention. Will you find your soulmate as you let the next Netflix special rollover? Probably not. But if you went out to a comedy show, maybe you have to share a table with someone. It is easy to turn to the screens when we are looking for love, but the best places to find people who are interested in the things that you are is to go out to them. Go to games, bookstores, or gallery openings, and see who else is there. Others will see you out and about. When you go out and do what you love, you are sending out the vibe of "I'm open to meeting new people," which will make people gravitate toward you. Do what you love, and like-minded people will find you.

Chapter 7:
How to Check If It Is Working

There may be a point where you feel stuck. It may feel like you have been meditating every day, and your manifestation isn't coming fast enough. There are a few things you could be doing wrong that are still preventing you from manifesting your desires. Remember that you create the life you want with what you believe in. Your beliefs can also thwart that life.

Our brains love being comfortable. Even if that means we become stagnant or continue bad habits that limit our growth. People who have been in unhealthy relationships keep "finding" themselves in unhealthy relationships. That's because their brains are used to it, even to that individual's detriment. Sometimes we find pleasure in the bad habits or limiting beliefs that we have. The more we believe them, the less we have to change, and change is hard. Growth and change put us at risk for struggles. True growth feels like a burning workout. It was painful, but there is pleasure in knowing you are getting stronger. Growing isn't painless, but it is exponentially rewarding.

Points of Self- Sabotage

Consistency

You can't meditate for 20 minutes one day a week and think that your manifestation is going to come. Manifesting is consistent practice. It has to be something you do throughout your day every day until it comes to you. You can allocate specific times throughout your day to pause and manifest. Manifestation isn't a fad diet. It is a new way of living and needs to become a new routine in your day, the way brushing your hair is. The law of attraction is a lifelong practice.

Not Being Grateful Enough

Gratitude is the number one way to accelerate your manifestations. If you aren't grateful for what you already have, the universe won't continue to supply all of the good things to you. Maybe a gratitude practice isn't clicking for you. Take a different approach or gratitude exercise and practice it for a week. See if your manifestations begin to appear once you take a new approach on gratitude. Once you have what you have desired, you need to up the levels of appreciation and acts of kindness. Tell your partner, family, and friends that you are grateful for them every day. Say thank you for your dream job every time you open the door to your office. Say thank you when you are lying on the beach in the Bahamas. Give more to charity, the more money you make.

Not Truly Believing

If you are consistently meditating and manifesting, but you aren't feeling or envisioning your desires, they won't come to you. Your brain believes whatever you put into your mind. If you continue to feel that these are nice thoughts, but they still aren't meant for you, then they aren't meant for you. Truly take the time to create that image and make your manifestation as detailed as possible. Any time you have a limiting thought, contradict it with a positive one and say the positive one more until you believe it. Then sit in it and feel it to the smallest sensory detail.

Holding onto Your Limiting Beliefs

It will be harder to manifest your desires when you are still holding onto limiting beliefs. These beliefs are pervasive and have been planted in us since we were born. It does take time to extract them out of your subconscious mind completely. Limiting beliefs are wired within us. When we continue to think the same thoughts, we are strengthening neural pathways. Neural pathways that are activated more frequently are triggered more easily. When you have a limiting belief race through your head, you have to actively rewire it. The limiting belief will still get triggered, but you being able to recognize it and taking control is what matters. When you have a limiting belief, immediately pause it and rewrite it.

Instead of letting a thought like, "I'll never be a good enough comic to go to festivals," take over, follow it with, "That isn't true. I have more than enough talent and potential and ambition to go to festivals. I have to prioritize it more."

The more you believe in yourself and tell yourself these positive affirmations, the easier those will become triggered. The less you think your limiting beliefs, the harder it will be to trigger them.

Not Being Ready to Receive It

Not being ready to receive your manifestation is a specific limiting believe. If you feel as though you aren't ready, the universe will listen to you. When you tell the universe you are ready, it will also listen to you. The universe will supply your desires the more you believe in them and say you are ready. You must rewire this limiting belief the way you do all the others.

Comparing Yourself To Others

Everyone's progress is at a different speed. Just because they have what you want doesn't mean that they are happy with it. There may be unintended consequences to what they have accomplished. Their spouse may seem perfect, but maybe they are being cheated on. Their job may be what you want, but it could be making them miserable. Their house looks incredible, but it could be out of their financial means. We don't know what lengths that person went to get to where they are today. It is healthy to have goals, but comparing and idolizing others sets us back. It makes us feel inadequate and puts more mental blocks around us and holds back our true potential. The more authentic and true you are to yourself, the more you will be able to manifest. Don't judge yourself for going down a different road. You are going down your own path, and that will look different from other people. Those who continue to walk down the well-paved path don't end up anywhere different. If you have a different destination, you have to walk there on your own and make it as you go (Martin, 2019).

Signs That Your Manifestation is Coming

You Feel Better Every Day

You will start to feel better and more confident the more positive words you add to your day. If you wake up and aren't dreading your morning, wishing you could sleep in, and are motivated to get the day started, then you know that your manifestations are starting to work. You feel better about your body image, your home, and those in your life. You start to see all of the beauty around you at more intense levels. The parts of your life that once bothered you seem to not get to you as easily anymore. The negatives don't seem so bad and don't seem as challenging. You feel like you can handle anything. You are less resistant to change and see something different as an opportunity to learn instead of something to shy away from ("11 Signs the Law of Attraction is Working, n.d).

Your Manifestations Start Happening Faster

The more you practice clearing your emotional path and raising your frequency, the faster your manifestations will come. This only happens through consistent practice, moments of gratitude, and constant reframing of limiting beliefs. After a while, manifestations will feel like riding a bicycle: effortless and enjoyable.

You Are More Present

The gratitude practices and mindfulness meditations will help you become more present. Your brain will stop bouncing back and forth between the past and the future. Your brain will start to quiet. It becomes easier for you to reshift your mind to the now when you notice it beginning to feel fragmented. You will be able to enjoy the present moment fully for what it is and be able to express gratitude for it.

Good Things Keep Happening

You start to notice these positive energies trickle into all aspects of your life. You are meeting more like-minded people; you get better job opportunities; your body has more energy; you have daily motivation for your goals. That is how you know that your negative energies have been removed. You are on the path for ultimate manifestation.

You Start Seeing Obstacles as Ways to Learn

You will begin to appreciate obstacles more than you ever have once you start aligning your energies. As we continue to raise our energy and remove our limiting beliefs, the universe might continue to throw those limiting beliefs at us because they are still in our subconscious. But it becomes easier for you to navigate through these obstacles, see them as areas of growth, self-sooth, and continue manifesting. You will be able to identify these lessons faster and rework them into your positive narrative for the day.

You Feel at Peace

You no longer feel like every day is a fight. You have confidence that the universe will take care of you and help you once you have aligned yourself with your manifestation desires. You feel a constant calm inside of you.

Conclusion

The rewards you receive when you faithfully and positively practice the law of attraction are endless. You have been given real stories of real people's lives who have actively used the law of attraction to create the life they deeply desired.

Hundreds of the most successful people currently and throughout the world are actively using the law of attraction this very moment. They have cut down their limiting beliefs and have channeled their energy towards positive actions and intentions.

The influence of the law of attraction is equally limitless. There are many more celebrities that have used the law of attraction, and this law has been a testament of religious philosophies over thousands of years. There are countless children's books, movies, and songs that all share one sounding truth: believe in yourself.

Once you commit yourself to the law of attraction, you will start to see life in it's full abundance. You will have endless energy to achieve your dreams. Each morning you will be filled with joy, regardless of what happened yesterday. The internal struggles and external pressures no longer seem to bother you. You notice the impermeable walls that you once had around you fall to the side.

The message of the law of attraction needs to be shared. This secret is no longer meant to be kept on people's shelves or hidden in attics. No one should live a life of suffering and no one should live a stagnant life. The chances of your life happening are so rare and improbable that you should desire to live the best life imaginable. Your dream life is all within you. You deserve happiness. You were born to have a positive and compassionate impact on this world.

Now that you have the tools, you can go out and start drawing your destiny. No one else can write your story but you.

Let's end this journey together with a success story. A reader of this book, who looks an awful lot like you, downloads this ebook. They aren't spiritual, but they are curious about the law of attraction. They read this book from start to finish and are endlessly inspired by the stories and destinies that have been influenced because of the law of attraction. They sit down and begin writing out their true dreams: where they want to live, their dream job, family life, and ideal relationship. They set intentional time aside each day to manifest the life they want. They are focused, calm, and positive while doing so. After some time passes, they begin to see more positive things happen to them. They get a promotion; they purchase a bigger house; they find their soulmate. Each day and after each event they practice gratitude. They give thanks for all that is in their lives and continue to pass on acts of kindness. Their attitude becomes infectious, and they positively impact other people's lives.

References

21 Positive Love Affirmations To Attract Love. (n.d.). Retrieved from https://www.self-help-and-self-development.com/love-affirmations.html.

Baker, B., Baker, B. B. B., Brendan, Akinlabi, M., Baker, B., Dunley, S., ... Education Essays. (2017, January 17). Top 100 Positive Affirmations for 2017. Retrieved from https://www.startofhappiness.com/positive-affirmations/.

Cole, Terri. (2017, May 4) 11 Questions to Clarify Your Beliefs About Love. *Positively Positive*, www.positivelypositive.com/2012/10/12/11-questions-to-clarify-your-beliefs-about-love/.

Crosby, Ruthanne, et al. (2018, November 8) The Important Law of Attraction Step Most People Leave Out. *Apply the Law of Attraction,*, www.applythelawofattraction.com/gratitude-law-attraction/

History of the Law of Attraction. (n.d.). Retrieved from https://thelawofattraction.org/history-of-the-law-of-attraction/

How the Teachings of the Bible are Related to the Law of Attraction. (2018, February 26). Retrieved from https://www.applythelawofattraction.com/teachings-bible-related-law-attraction/.

Hurst, K., & Hurst, K. (2019, April 16). 10 Gratitude Exercises You Should Try Today For Increased Happiness. Retrieved from http://www.thelawofattraction.com/10-ways-to-increase-gratitude/

Hurst, K., & Hurst, K. (2019, June 11). How To Manifest Love With A Specific Person Using The Law Of Attraction. Retrieved from http://www.thelawofattraction.com/how-to-manifest-love/.

Hurst, K., & Hurst, K. (2018, May 18). Best Law Of Attraction Videos: Oprah Winfrey And The Law Of Attraction. Retrieved from http://www.thelawofattraction.com/oprah-winfrey-credits-the-law-of-attraction-for-her-success-in-revealing-interview/.

Hurst, K., & Hurst, K. (2019, April 15). Is It Really Possible To Manifest Money? 10 Steps To Manifesting Money. Retrieved from www.thelawofattraction.com/really-possible-manifest-money/.

Hurst, K., & Hurst, K. (2019, April 3). How To Keep To A Diet: 4 Ways To Make Healthy Eating A Daily Habit. Retrieved from http://www.thelawofattraction.com/4-ways-make-healthy-eating-daily-habit/.

Living the Law of Attraction. (n.d.). Retrieved from https://www.oprah.com/spirit/the-law-of-attraction-real-life-stories_1/all#ixzz62BE4rTXw.

Martin. (2019, April 8). Self Sabotage And The Subconscious Mind. Retrieved from https://www.eruptingmind.com/self-sabotage-the-subconscious-mind/.

Novak, M. (2019, September 3). 62 Self-Limiting Beliefs that Block Happiness and Success • Believe and Create. Retrieved from https://believeandcreate.com/62-beliefs-that-limit-your-happiness-and-success/.

PowerofPositivity. (2019, April 18) 11 Signs The Law of Attraction Is Working For You. *Power of Positivity: Positive Thinking & Attitude*, www.powerofpositivity.com/11-signs-law-attraction-working/.

Sicinski, A., & Adam, A. S. (2018, December 6). The Complete Guide on How to Overcome Your Limiting Beliefs. Retrieved from https://blog.iqmatrix.com/limiting-beliefs.

Tops, Charlene. (2014, April 11) Stop Sabotaging Yourself in 5 Easy Steps. *Lifehack*, Lifehack, www.lifehack.org/articles/communication/stop-sabotaging-yourself-5-easy-steps.html.

Why Is It Hard to Live for the Moment. (n.d.). Retrieved from https://www.psychologytoday.com/us/blog/feeling-smart/201609/why-is-it-hard-live-the-moment.

WakingTimes. (2016, June 18). 21 Ways to Raise Your Vibration. Retrieved from https://www.wakingtimes.com/2013/01/16/21-ways-to-raise-your-vibration/.

Printed in Great Britain
by Amazon